THE COLOURS
OF HISTORY

Clive Gifford

Illustrated by Marc-Etienne Peintre

Quarto is the authority on a wide range of topics.

Quarto educates, entertains and enriches the lives of our readers—enthusiasts and lovers of hands-on living.

www.quartoknows.com

© 2018 Quarto Publishing plc

First Published in 2018 by QED Publishing
an imprint of The Quarto Group.
The Old Brewery, 6 Blundell Street,
London N7 9BH, United Kingdom.
T (0)20 7700 6700 F (0)20 7700 8066
www.QuartoKnows.com

A catalogue record for this book is available from the British Library.

ISBN 978-1-78493-967-0

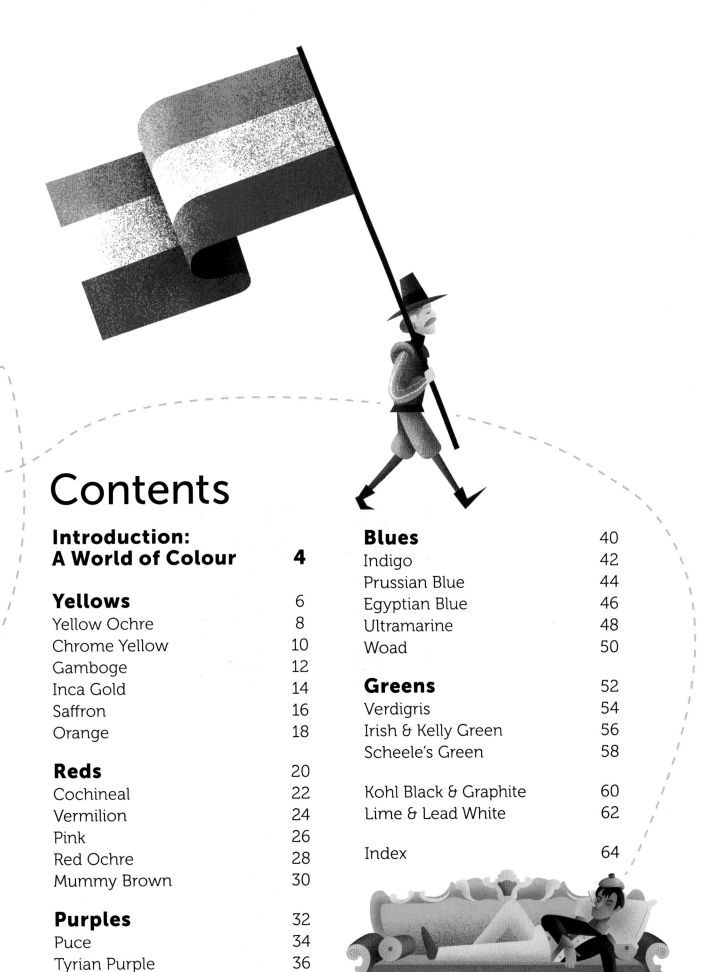

Contents

Introduction
A World of Colour

Imagine a world without colour. How drab and dreary it would seem!
No glowing red and yellow sunsets or brilliant green fields and forests.
From showing our support for a particular sports team by wearing its
colours, to recognising red or green signals at traffic lights, colour plays
a part in everything we do.

The colours of nature

Colour has always played a crucial role in the natural world. Some living creatures use colours as camouflage, to hide among their surroundings. Others stand out in bright colours, which they use to attract mates or to warn other creatures away. Prehistoric peoples learned to recognise the colours of certain plants, fruits and berries. The colours helped them tell which were ripe and could be eaten, and which were harmful.

Colour crazes

Throughout history, many colours – both natural and synthetic – have stimulated the imagination. They have excited, outraged and inspired fashions and fads, from passions for pinks to crazes for particular purples, yellows or greens. Some sources of colour at certain points in history became as valuable as gold. A few were so highly prized that battles were fought over them!

A colourful history

This book contains a selection of colourful tales that will take you on a whirlwind journey to different places at different times in history. As some pigments have given rise to a range of shades, we have handpicked a sample of each tale's colour to show a typical example. Along the way, you'll discover many of the ingenious ways people have obtained colours, how some shades were lost then rediscovered, and how their use was sometimes spread by traders, explorers and conquerors. You'll learn how the colour orange was adopted by the Dutch, how a river flows bright green every year in Chicago, how it took thousands of sea snails just to dye a single purple robe...and much more besides!

Yellow is one of the three primary colours of paints and pigments, along with blue and red. Throughout history, it has been thought of as the colour of sunshine and warmth in many cultures and was so prized in Imperial China that only the country's Emperor and Empress could wear certain yellow shades. But yellow also has a dark side. It is the colour of cowardice to many and to some, the colour of sickness, possibly because of the yellowing of the skin caused by diseases such as jaundice and malaria.

Yellows

Yellow Ochre

Chrome Yellow

Gamboge

Inca Gold

Saffron

Orange

Yellow Ochre

In 1940, four teenagers were exploring the woods near their home town of Montignac, France, when one of them made an astonishing discovery. A deep hole led the boys into the previously unknown Lascaux Cave. Its walls were covered in colourful prehistoric cave art, much of it painted in yellow ochre.

Clay colour

Yellow ochre is an earthy pigment made from clay containing iron oxide. This clay is found in many places in the world, and early people ground it down into a powder. Mixing the powder with plant sap or water made paint that could be dabbed onto rock using hands, leaves, tree bark or thin animal bones. At Lascaux, some of the artwork was spray-painted onto the rock walls by blowing paint through a reed or hollow bone.

Made to last

The paintings discovered by the teenagers featured yellows and reds made from ochre. There was also black, which came from charcoal. The paintings depicted more than 2,000 different figures, mostly animals such as horses, bulls and stags – and even a rhinoceros! Unlike some other pigments, yellow ochre does not decay or fade quickly, especially when it is not exposed to sunlight. Many of Lascaux's cave paintings are thought to be more than 17,000 years old.

Around the world

Royal tombs in ancient Egypt were often decorated with yellow ochre walls, and Australian Aboriginals painted with it, too. It was later used by many famous artists including Rembrandt, Renoir and Raphael. By the 18th century, France had become a centre for the production of yellow ochre. The Huli tribe in Papua New Guinea and the Fulani people in western Africa still work with yellow ochre, using it as make-up for ceremonies, covering their entire face in the colour.

Chrome Yellow

In the early 1760s, a French geologist found a new mineral lurking deep within a Russian gold mine. He named it 'crocoite'. It would give rise to a stunningly bright yellow colour seized upon by a young, struggling painter: Vincent Van Gogh. He used it to produce some of his most memorable works of art.

It's elementary!

French chemist Nicolas-Louis Vauquelin experimented on crocoite and discovered a new chemical element. He called it 'chromium', after the Greek for 'colour'. Vauquelin discovered that a combination of chromium and lead produced a vivid yellow colour. It soon became a popular ingredient in artists' paints. King George IV of England liked it so much that he had much of his seaside retreat, The Royal Pavilion at Brighton, decorated using the colour.

Bright lights

Chrome yellow's bright yellow-orange hue was a hit with French painters such as Claude Monet and Paul Cézanne. Vincent Van Gogh's early paintings were dull and drab, but after being inspired by others' bright artworks, he began working in feverishly bright colours. He used chrome yellow extensively on a series of paintings of sunflowers and wheatfields. Nearly a century after it was painted, one of his paintings of sunflowers sold for US$39.7 million!

Browned off

It eventually became clear that over long periods of time, chrome yellow changed under light, slowly turning to a dull brown. This fate is befalling some of Van Gogh's paintings. Artists began switching to other yellows that didn't fade and change. However, this shade of yellow is still used for school buses in the United States, as well as yellow lines and other road markings.

A colour to make you go
Gamboge

Gamboge got its name from the country of Cambodia, which was once known as Camboja. The colour was used as a paint in China, Japan and India for over 800 years before it reached Europe.

Special sap

Gamboge was made from the garcinia trees which are found in Cambodia, Sri Lanka and Thailand. Collectors would make a deep cut into the trunk of a mature tree and place a hollowed-out piece of bamboo to channel the milky sap that flowed out. The sap was then roasted over a fire. It took a long time to harden into brown lumps that looked like toffee. At first glance it was far from inspiring, but as soon as water was added, it produced a warm, golden-yellow colour.

Painting plants

Gamboge was used by many painters in the 17th and 18th centuries, such as Pieter Breugel the Elder, Rembrandt and the famous English landscape artist, J.M.W. Turner. Another English artist, William Hooker, produced plant illustrations for scientists. He was desperate for a strong green that would let him accurately depict the colour of many plants' leaves. He mixed gamboge with Prussian blue (see pages 44–45) to produce a brand new colour – Hooker's green.

Medical moments

In 1603, a Dutch doctor and botanist, Carolus Clusius, obtained one of the first known samples of the pigment in Europe. It had been brought to Amsterdam from China by Dutch ships. For a time, gamboge became a popular medicine in Europe. It was used to treat rheumatism, scurvy and other illnesses. However, gamboge is poisonous and in large doses could be fatal. Even small doses act as a very powerful laxative! Workers at a London paint-making factory in the 19th century found that they had to go to the toilet every hour when handling gamboge.

The colour of plunder

Inca Gold

Gold has been highly prized by many civilizations, especially the Inca Empire. For the Incas, gold was connected to their sun god, Inti. But the precious metal's high value to European explorers and soldiers would hasten the Incas' downfall.

Mountain empire

At its peak, around 1500 CE, the Inca Empire covered much of western South America, stretching from Chile to Ecuador. This mountainous territory contained rich deposits of gold and silver. The Incas mined the gold, and also took it from peoples they conquered in battle. Ordinary Incas had to perform compulsory work – called *mit'a* – for their emperor. Some performed their *mit'a* by mining precious metals.

"Get gold, humanely, if you can, but at all hazards, get gold."

KING FERDINAND'S INSTRUCTIONS
TO SPANISH EXPLORERS, 1511

The sweat of the Sun

The Incas were incredibly skilled at working gold into beautiful and elaborate designs. They thought of this precious metal as the sweat of the Sun. All gold belonged by right to their ruler, the Sapa Inca. One Sapa Inca, Atahualpa, drank from gold cups, wore pure gold headdresses and jewellery – and even had a throne made of more than 70 kilograms of solid gold.

Greedy for gold

A Spanish soldier, Hernán Cortés, had claimed vast riches from the Aztec Empire in Mexico. Another Spaniard, Francisco Pizarro, wanted his own share of the spoils. In 1532 he arrived in Cajamarca with a force of just under 170 men. He was outnumbered, but the Incas had never seen horses or guns before, and many fled or were killed. Pizarro captured Atahualpa, who promised to fill a room with gold if his life was spared. Over seven tonnes of gold treasure were brought, but the Inca ruler was still executed. The years that followed saw thousands of Inca gold treasures seized, melted down and sent back to Spain.

The world's most expensive colour

Saffron

A rich golden yellow-orange colour, saffron comes from a particular species of crocus grown mostly in Iran and Spain. Delicate threads inside the flower give saffron its distinctive colour and flavour. In the past, it was much in demand as a dye and a medicine. It remains popular today as a food colouring and flavouring.

Worth its weight in gold?

To harvest just half a kilogram of saffron requires 55,000–85,000 flowers, so a single gram can cost as much as £15. Saffron's high price meant that in the past, it was used mostly by people of wealth and power. Alexander the Great is said to have bathed in saffron to heal wounds while the Roman emperor Nero used it as an air freshener. Saffron boiled in wine was piped into Rome's mighty Colosseum to mask the bloody stench of battling gladiators.

Colour crimes

Throughout medieval Europe, saffron was bought and traded – and sometimes stolen. Pirates hijacked ships carrying the precious cargo, and one such theft led to a three-month conflict called the Saffron War. Traders sometimes cheated by filling out their parcels of saffron with cheaper substances. In 1444, a trader in Germany who diluted his saffron with shredded marigold flowers was burned alive!

A holy colour

The robes of many Buddhist monks are dyed this colour, although using saffron itself was often too expensive. Instead, the monks used vegetable dyes made from a far cheaper spice, turmeric. Christian monks who produced prayer books by hand occasionally used saffron instead of real gold to illuminate letters. Hindus mix saffron into a coloured paste, used to make a mark called a *tilak* on the statues of deities. Saffron appears on the national flag of India, where it represents courage and sacrifice.

A colour to go mad for

Orange

Ancient Egyptians painted in orange using a ground-up mineral called realgar – a mixture of sulphur and poisonous arsenic. This pigment was also used in European painting, but orange remained a colour without a name in Europe for many centuries.

What's in a name?

Orange was simply known as 'yellow-red' in Europe until Portuguese and Italian traders returned from Asia in the 15th and 16th centuries, bringing home sweet orange trees. The colour took its name from the fruit, which was called *nāranga* in the Sanskrit language, becoming *naranja* in Spanish and eventually 'orange' in English and French.

House of Orange

Centuries before the colour got its name, a small independent state (now in southern France) was named 'Orange'. This state gave its name to the royal house of the Netherlands, and they adopted orange as their colour. The colour was widely used in paintings, and Dutch farmers managed to breed bright orange carrots. (Before that time, all carrots were purple or white.)

Orange madness

When the Dutch flag was first flown in the 1570s, it was orange, white and blue. But it's thought that the orange dyes of the time turned yellow or red after exposure to the sun and over time the orange was officially replaced by red. Even so, the Dutch people continue to celebrate orange, especially on *Koningsdag* – the birthday of the country's king. This national holiday features *Oranjegekte* ('orange madness') as crowds take to the streets, eating orange food and wearing orange clothes, hats and wigs.

High-vis tint

A colour that stands out even in poor light, today orange is used for lifejackets, safety signs and high visibility clothing. Aircraft 'black boxes' (which record flight details in case of a crash) are actually orange so they can be easily found among crash wreckage.

Love, anger, heat and passion.
Red is a colour with many meanings in
different cultures through history. The colour
of blood, it has been associated with courage
and sacrifice in some countries and with
happiness and joy in others. To the ancient
Romans, for example, it was the colour of
Mars, their god of war. This strong, attention-
grabbing colour is often found in warning
signs and used to symbolise danger.

Reds

Cochineal

Vermilion

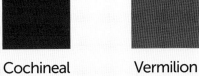

Pink

Red Ochre

Mummy Brown

Colour from cactus creatures
Cochineal

The cochineal is an insect smaller than your fingernail which lives off certain types of cacti. When squashed, the insect yields a vibrant scarlet red colour – caused by the carminic acid it carries in its body to keep ants from eating it.

Crushed creatures

It takes over 140,000 cochineal insects – dried in the sun and then crushed and ground – to make a single kilogram of the colour. Civilizations in the Americas, such as the Maya, Aztecs and Incas, used cochineal as a paint and dye to colour the robes of their leaders. When Spanish conquistadors invaded Mexico in 1519, they discovered cochineal for sale in Aztec markets. The Spanish invaders took over cochineal production, keeping its source secret while shipping hundreds of tonnes of it back to Europe. After gold and silver, cochineal became the most valuable product to come from the Americas. When local peoples were conquered, the Spanish could then control the supply of cochineal.

Ready for red

At that time, strong scarlet colours were a symbol of power in Europe, partly because long-lasting and intense red dyes were rare and expensive. In the time of Henry VI of England, a roll of scarlet cloth could cost three years' wages for an average worker. Cochineal's vivid red was used to make red velvet and to fashion the red robes of cardinals in the Roman Catholic church. It was later adopted by British Army officers, giving them the nickname 'redcoats'. Pirates targeted and robbed Spanish ships carrying cochineal.

Bugs in your food

Cochineal was overtaken by cheaper red colourings in the 19th century, but is still produced today, mostly in Peru. It is used in lipsticks and as a colouring in some ice creams, yoghurts and sweets, where it appears as 'E120' or 'natural red no. 4' on the list of ingredients.

The colour of victory
Vermilion

Beautiful but dangerous, vermilion's brilliant red colour came first from ground-down pieces of a mineral called cinnabar, which contains poisonous mercury and sulphur. It found favour among the great empires of Rome and China.

Winning colours

The ancient Romans got most of their cinnabar from mercury mines in central Spain. The prisoners who were forced to work there rarely lasted more than a couple of years before poisonous mercury fumes took their lives. Vermilion was in demand as a paint for wealthy villas and was sometimes used to colour the face or body of victorious generals or successful gladiators as they paraded through Rome.

An explosion of colour

Alchemists tried to turn metals and other substances into precious gold. Some found ways of making vermilion without cinnabar by heating a mixture of sulphur and mercury. However, the potential for explosions and poisonous fumes made it dangerous. Despite the risk, there was steady demand for a bright red colour to illuminate religious manuscripts. It was often covered in a glaze made from egg white mixed with human earwax.

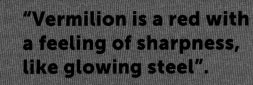

Chinese red

Red was a vital colour in ancient China, where it signified blood and life. Vermilion, from both ground cinnabar and through mixing substances, was known there as 'Chinese red'. It was mixed with sap from the lacquer tree to produce a waterproof, plastic-like finish to bowls and boxes. The colour was also used to create red seals for official messages and documents, and many Chinese temples were painted in vivid vermilion. Special vermilion ink was produced for use solely by the emperor to mark official documents.

Pink

Long ago, 'pink' was actually the name for a kind of yellow, which was made from the bark of an oak tree. It wasn't until the 17th and 18th centuries that it started to become the name of the popular pale red colour.

Pink for boys

For centuries, pink was worn by both men and women. In some eras, it became more popular with one gender or the other. For example, in 18th century France, the famous socialite Madame de Pompadour inspired a craze for light pink clothing and china. In some societies in the 19th and early 20th centuries, pink was reserved for young boys, not girls. Red was thought of as a strong, manly colour, and as pink came from red mixed with white, it was not thought of as suitable for delicate girls.

Pink on toast

In the 1860s, Emperor Napoleon III of France offered a prize to anyone who could make a cheap butter substitute for his armies. One French chemist responded by inventing margarine. Margarine was naturally white, so was dyed yellow to make it look more like butter. In the US, this angered the butter industry. By 1902, 32 states had passed laws either banning yellow margarine or forcing it to be coloured bright pink to distinguish it from butter.

"Pink, being a more decided and stronger color, is more suitable for the boy".

A US TRADE MAGAZINE FOR BABY CLOTHES MANUFACTURERS, JUNE 1918

Popular pink

In the 1950s, pink's popularity with girls and women was helped by the US president's wife. Mamie Eisenhower often wore pink dresses on public occasions and decorated the White House in the colour so much that it was nicknamed 'the Pink Palace'. In the 1930s, Italian fashion designer Else Schiaparelli developed a bold shade known as 'shocking' or 'hot' pink. It was hugely popular with teenagers in the 1950s and 1960s.

Prehistoric paint

Red Ochre

In South Africa's Blombos Cave, archaeologists found the world's oldest known paint box. There were blocks of red ochre rock carved with patterns, seashells containing traces of red ochre, stones used for grinding the ochre down into powder and simple mixing tools made of bone. They are all around 70,000 to 100,000 years old.

Rusty red

Red ochre is mostly made up of a mineral called haematite. It is found widely on the Earth's surface, and underground as well. Lion's Cavern in the African country of Swaziland contains a red ochre mine that is 43,000 years old. Prehistoric people used chunks of red ochre to draw directly on stone. They also ground it down and mixed it with animal fats or sap from plants. These acted as a binder, to make the colour stick to surfaces.

Art all over

Red ochre art is found all over the world, from cave paintings in France and Spain to Aboriginal art sites in Australia. One cave in Argentina contains dozens of hand shapes in red ochre. They were made over 7,000 years ago by stencilling on the rock. Red ochre was used by the Mesopotamians to dye cloth. Centuries later, European artists such as Michelangelo and Vermeer used it to produce warm red colours in their paintings.

Painted people

Many different peoples used red ochre as body paint. These included the Picts in Scotland and the Maasai and Himba peoples of Africa. In Newfoundland, Canada, the Beothuk people mixed red ochre with grease from the caribou they hunted, then covered themselves in red ochre paint. Because of its blood-like colour, red ochre was sometimes used in death or burial ceremonies. The bones of a 33,000-year-old skeleton found in England were dyed bright red with the colour. Other red-dyed skeletons, many thousands of years old, have been found in Mexico, Russia and around the Mediterranean.

A colour with a past life
Mummy Brown

The ancient Egyptians mummifed people, cats and other animals. Some of these were also ground down to make mummy brown.

When ancient Egyptians preserved the bodies of their dead for the afterlife, they sometimes waterproofed them with bitumen, a thick, oily black form of petroleum that oozes up from cracks in the ground.

Flash-forward a few thousand years, and the Egyptian mummies were no longer enjoying an untroubled afterlife. A passion for a particular shade of brown had gripped artists in Europe from the 1500s onwards. Not all knew that it actually contained the remains of real Egyptian mummies, ground up and mixed with oils and plant extracts. It was the bitumen in the mummies that created the brown colour.

In demand

The demand for ancient Egyptian mummies saw thousands shipped to Europe. Some were to make paint, but others were put on display or used as medicine. Ground-up mummy powder was thought by many to cure all sorts of ills, from headaches to stomach ulcers.

Laid to rest

Mummy brown fell out of fashion in the late 1800s, when some artists learned what they were painting with. When the pre-Raphaelite painter Edward Burne-Jones discovered the news in 1881, he immediately gave his tubes of paint a burial in his garden. Even so, the colour continued to be sold until the 1960s, when a famous London paint supplier reported that they'd run out of mummies.

Royalty, power and privilege. Purple has long been a colour connected with luxury and prestige, partly because it is one of the rarest colours in the natural world. It was first used by French cave painters more than 20,000 years ago, creating pigments from ground-down hematite or manganese ores. It has since been made in a variety of ways from mixing chemicals in laboratories to extracting the colour from plant roots and sea creatures.

Purples

Puce

Tyrian Purple

Orchil

A colour fit for a queen
Puce

Puce is a mysterious colour that not even dictionaries agree on – is it purple, brown or grey? No one knows exactly who first came up with the precise shade, either. One thing we do know is that it owes its name to the last queen of France, Marie-Antoinette.

A passion for fashion

Marie-Antoinette married the future King Louis XVI of France when she was only fourteen. At first, she was adored by the French people, but over time, many turned against her. This was partly due to her wild shopping sprees – the queen would have eighteen pairs of new gloves delivered each week or wear three different outfits per day. Each dress was staggeringly expensive. Her nickname among the French people became 'Madame Deficit'.

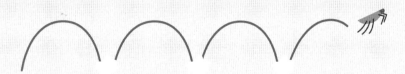

Flea fashion?

The king walked in on Marie one day to see her trying on yet another expensive gown. It was made of silk in a purple-pink-brown colour. The king tried to put her off the purchase by declaring it to be *couleur de puce* – the colour of a flea after it had been squashed! Marie-Antoinette wasn't put off. She insisted that every lady in her court wore puce or subtly similar shades known as *dos de puce* (flea's back) or *ventre de puce* (flea's belly). When an English noblewoman visited later in 1775, she wrote that, "You can wear no colour that is not either *dos de puce* or *ventre de puce*; it is uniform at Fontainebleau and the only colour that can be worn."

Losing her head

Long after the fashion for puce moved on, unrest in France led to a revolution. The king and queen were overthrown and Marie-Antoinette was beheaded in 1793. Although rather unloved and under-used, puce lived on and is still occasionally used in clothing and furnishings.

A colour fit for royalty

Tyrian Purple

Three thousand years ago, the people of Tyre, a coastal city in what is now Lebanon, discovered how the clear, slimy mucus of sea snails turned into a strong purple dye, once exposed to air and sunlight. This Tyrian purple didn't fade and became highly prized for its strength and rarity. In this way, the slimy snails helped to build a mighty trading empire.

Vast numbers of snails were collected, their shells cracked and then left to rot in the sun. According to ancient authors, the stench was awful. It took more than 9,000 sea snails just to make one single gram of the dye – not even enough to colour an entire dress. This made the dye phenomenally costly. By 300 CE, Tyrian purple was three times more expensive than pure gold.

Purple power

The ancient Romans were particularly partial to purple. At first, conquering generals would return in triumph wearing purple cloaks while Roman politicians would wear a band of purple on their bright, white togas. In the later Roman Empire, only Emperors and statues of Roman gods were allowed to dress in the colour. According to Roman historian Suetonius, in 40 CE, the Emperor Caligula was so angered at a visiting ruler, Ptolemy of Mauretania, wearing a more splendid purple cloak, that he had the visiting king murdered.

Perkin's purple

Tyrian purple continued to be very expensive until an 18-year-old English chemist, William Henry Perkin made an accidental discovery in 1856. While trying to invent a drug to tackle the deadly disease of malaria, Perkin ended up with an artificial purple dye. After Empress Eugenie of France and Britain's Queen Victoria adopted the colour for their gowns, it became the height of fashion in Europe and the United States.

"It brightens every garment, and shares with gold the glory of the triumph."

ROMAN WRITER PLINY THE ELDER (23–79 CE)

The poor man's purple
Orchil

In ancient Rome, most ordinary people could only dream of clothing dyed in costly Tyrian purple. But some could lay their hands on a cheaper alternative, made from lichens found on rocks. This colour was known as orchil, archil or orchell.

Smelly work

Orchil ranged from a dark red to a strong purple, but creating the colour took a long time and was unpleasant work. The lichens had to be harvested at just the right time of year, ground down and mixed with potash and stale human urine. The stinking mixture then had to be kneaded like bread dough. In some recipes, it was left for a long and smelly time – up to 70 days – before the dye was ready to use.

Orchil trade

Orchil was sometimes used as a base dye on a piece of purple cloth. A smaller amount of expensive Tyrian purple was then used to complete the cloth. Some traders tricked customers by selling them orchil instead of Tyrian purple. Orchil went out of fashion for a while, until the Middle Ages, when traders from Italy reintroduced the dye after collecting samples from the Middle East. A family from Florence controlled trade in the dye for a century in parts of Europe. It was in demand to colour wool and silk.

Cudbear

In the 1750s, George and Cuthbert Gordon developed a new method of making orchil in Scotland. It allowed them to produce 78 different shades. They called their dye 'cudbear'. They kept their methods top secret, building a high wall around their Glasgow factory. Business was so good that supplies of lichens in Scotland ran out, and they had to import more than 200 tonnes each year from Norway and Sweden.

"Mr Gordon ought to be encouraged by every lover of his country for such a curious and valuable improvement".

THE SCOTS MAGAZINE ABOUT CUDBEAR, 1776

The colour of the sea and sky, shades of
blue have been part of art for thousands
of years. Considered cold and calm
compared to fiery red, blue is the colour
of trust, excellence and performance in
business. Blue is also associated with
sadness and is sometimes used to represent
ghosts in Japanese kabuki theatre.
In Thailand, blue is the colour of Friday,
with light blue being considered lucky.

Blues

Indigo

Prussian
Blue

Egyptian
Blue

Ultramarine

Woad

The colour of cool

Indigo

Known as *nila* in India, meaning 'dark blue', natural indigo comes from plants which grow in Asia as well as South and Central America. When left to rot and then mixed with liquid, the plants' green-blue leaves would turn cloth and yarn yellow. Then, after being exposed to air, they turn blue.

Blue planet

Indigo proved very popular worldwide. Indigo has been found in ancient Egyptian tombs and in historic Japanese art, while the oldest known indigo object is a piece of dyed cotton cloth from Peru which is over 6,000 years old. When a boy becomes a man among the Tuareg peoples of North Africa, he is given a precious indigo headscarf called a *tagelmust* to protect him against heat and sandstorms in the desert.

The indigo trade

After Portuguese explorer Vasco da Gama discovered a sea route from Europe to Asia in the 1490s, a great trade in indigo began. India was the centre of production but plantations also sprang up in the New World (the Americas) to fulfil demand.

SALOON

"I make no doubt indigo will prove a very valuable Commodity in time."

ELIZA LUCAS, US INDIGO PLANTATION OWNER IN THE 1740s

Jeans genius

Indigo was used to colour a type of cloth in the French city of Nîmes. It was called *serge de Nîmes*, which over time was simplified to 'denim'. Levi Strauss and Jacob Davis began fashioning it into hardwearing work clothes for miners and cowboys in America's Wild West. These caught on, and a multi-billion dollar industry was born. The word 'jeans' comes from the French word for people from Genoa in Italy where another blue cloth was produced, also created using indigo.

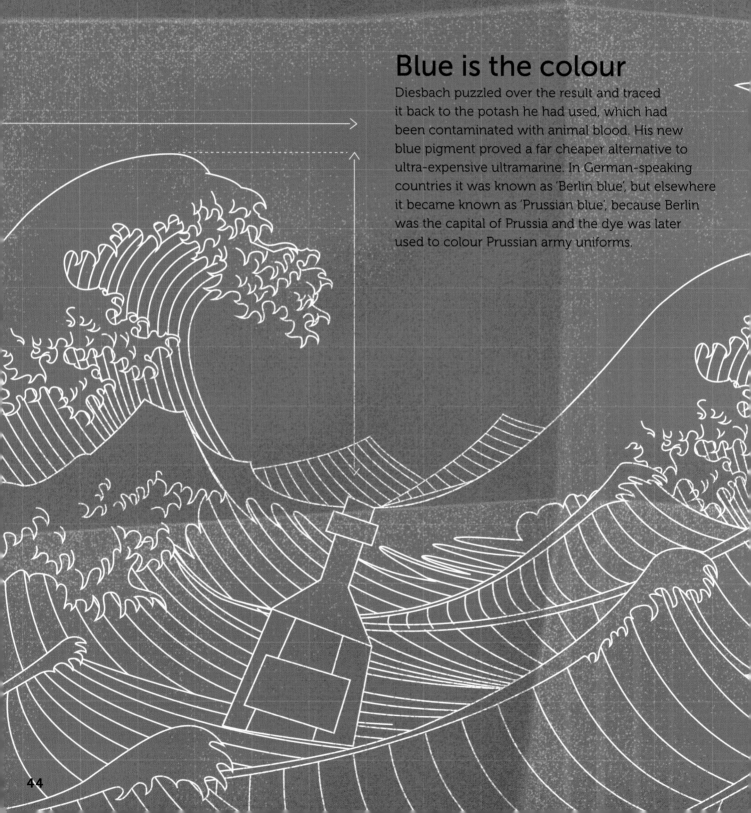

An accidental colour

Prussian Blue

One day in the early 18th century, Berlin-based paint maker Johann Diesbach was trying to make a rich, red pigment called 'Florentine Lake'. But something went wrong, and his stew of iron sulphate, potash and crushed cochineal insects resulted in a purple colour which boiled down to a rich, dark blue.

Blue is the colour

Diesbach puzzled over the result and traced it back to the potash he had used, which had been contaminated with animal blood. His new blue pigment proved a far cheaper alternative to ultra-expensive ultramarine. In German-speaking countries it was known as 'Berlin blue', but elsewhere it became known as 'Prussian blue', because Berlin was the capital of Prussia and the dye was later used to colour Prussian army uniforms.

Paint and ink

Prussian blue mixed well with other colours and was used by many artists including Van Gogh and Picasso. When the colour was exported to Japan in the 19th century, it caused a sensation. The colour was used heavily by famous woodblock print artists such as Katsushika Hokusai, who used it for the colour of the sea. It was also used to produce black and blue printing inks.

Blueprints

More than a century after its discovery, the chemist and astronomer John Herschel invented an early form of photocopying by plunging light-sensitive paper into a bath of Prussian blue. Architects and engineers could draw one set of plans on tracing paper and quickly make copies. The lines drawn on the tracing paper kept light from travelling through, but the blank parts let light reach the copy paper below. The paper then turned blue, leaving a copy of the drawing in white. These copies were called blueprints.

The colour of the Nile
Egyptian Blue

The ancient Roman city of Pompeii lay undisturbed for over 1,600 years after being buried in a volcanic eruption in 79 CE. When it was finally uncovered, one of the first artificial colours was discovered on the city's walls and in paint bowls. It was named after its inventors, the ancient Egyptians.

The colour of the heavens

Blue was an incredibly important colour to the ancient Egyptians. It was the colour of the sky and of the River Nile, upon which the Egyptians depended for water, fish and transport. Blue was associated with their gods, the universe and creation. The only problem was that the Egyptians had access to few blue pigments apart from lapis lazuli, which was rare and expensive.

Sophisticated system

Around 4,600 years ago, the Egyptians worked out how to make a pigment out of rocks and minerals. Quartz sand, copper ore and other materials were all heated together at high temperatures – usually 850–950°C – for several days. This new colour proved incredibly long-lasting, and it could be made lighter in colour by grinding it down into a fine powder.

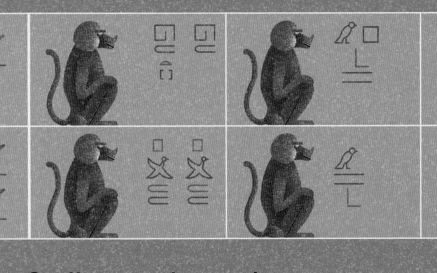

Scribes and scarabs

Scribes in ancient Egypt kept records of harvests, taxes and other government business on papyrus scrolls. They wrote using brushes made from frayed reeds dipped in Egyptian blue. The colour was also used as a shiny glaze on objects such as jewellery, often featuring the scarab beetle, which was thought to ward off evil.

Blue baboons

In the tombs of Egyptian pharaohs and nobles, the walls were covered with smooth plaster. Artists painted scenes on them, often featuring Egyptian blue. For instance, twelve Egyptian blue baboon monkeys grace the most famous tomb of all – that of the young pharaoh Tutankhamun. They represent the twelve hours it was believed it would take the dead pharaoh to travel to the afterlife.

A colour made from gem stones
Ultramarine

The deepest and most vivid of blues, ultramarine is made from ground-down lapis lazuli. This semi-precious stone has decorated the coffins and death masks of ancient Egyptian pharaohs such as King Tutankhamun.

Beyond the seas

Ultramarine gets its name from the Latin for 'beyond the seas'. During the Renaissance, lapis lazuli had to come all the way from Afghanistan to Europe – carried overland by donkeys and then shipped across the Mediterranean Sea. It then had to be ground down, mixed with wax, pine resin and oils, before being heated and kneaded for hours, like bread dough. All this added up to make ultramarine at least 100 times the price of other paint colours.

Artist angst

Despite its expense, some customers insisted on ultramarine. In Europe, it coloured the deep blue robes worn by the Virgin Mary in religious paintings. Artists often had to haggle with their clients over how much of the colour they could use. The Dutch painter Johannes Vermeer used ultramarine heavily to produce some extraordinary paintings, even though he had to take out loans to cover the costs. When he died, his family were left heavily in debt.

Prize-winning paint

In 1824, an industrial organization in France offered a huge reward for anyone who could develop an artificial ultramarine. French chemist Jean-Baptiste Guimet won the prize, and his synthetic ultramarine is now used as an affordable art colour. Impressionist painters including Renoir and Monet and 20th century artists like Yves Klein worked heavily in synthetic ultramarine. Klein liked it so much that he developed his own ultramarine shade, now known as IKB (International Klein Blue).

> "Illustrious, beautiful, and most perfect, beyond all other colours."
>
> ITALIAN ARTIST CENNINO CENNINI, 15TH CENTURY

The blue of battle
Woad

A plant called woad grows throughout Europe. Its pretty yellow flowers bloom in fields and meadows, but its crushed leaves make a strong blue dye. It was used to colour cloth and some people – such as Celts in ancient Britain – applied it as a war paint.

Woad rage

In 60 CE, large parts of England were under the rule of the ancient Romans. Queen Boudicca of the Iceni tribe led a fierce rebellion in eastern England. She is said to have daubed her face with woad before going into battle. Other Celts covered their bodies in woad, possibly because it acts as an antiseptic – so it may have helped prevent infections in wounds. Boudicca's forces won several important battles before she was finally defeated by the Romans.

"All the Britons dye their bodies with woad, which produces a blue colour, and this gives them a more terrifying appearance in battle."

ROMAN LEADER JULIUS CAESAR, ABOUT 54 CE

Leafy blue

Centuries after Boudicca's death, woad continued to be made in similar ways. Leaves were harvested, ground down and formed into balls which were left for two or three months. Water was added to help the woad ferment. When it was ready, the woad would be dried and sold to cloth dyers. Before the arrival of indigo, it was the main blue colourant available in Europe, so it was used by many peoples including the Anglo-Saxons, Franks, Vandals and Vikings.

Blue gold

In the Middle Ages, producing and dyeing with woad formed a huge, profitable industry. It made Coventry one of the largest cities in Britain, and woad merchants became wealthy and powerful. When indigo (see pages 42–43) threatened woad's dominance, it was denounced as 'the Devil's dye'. In 1609, the French king protected the woad industry by sentencing to death anyone who was caught using indigo.

Green is the colour most closely associated with nature. Chlorophyll gives plants their green colour, and the ancient Egyptian symbol for the colour was a stalk of the papyrus plant. Today, 'green' parties and organisations campaign to conserve the environment. Green is considered the colour of spring and newness – and envy, too. William Shakespeare coined the phrase 'green-eyed monster' to describe jealousy in his play, *Othello*.

Greens

Verdigris

Irish and
Kelly Green

Scheele's Green

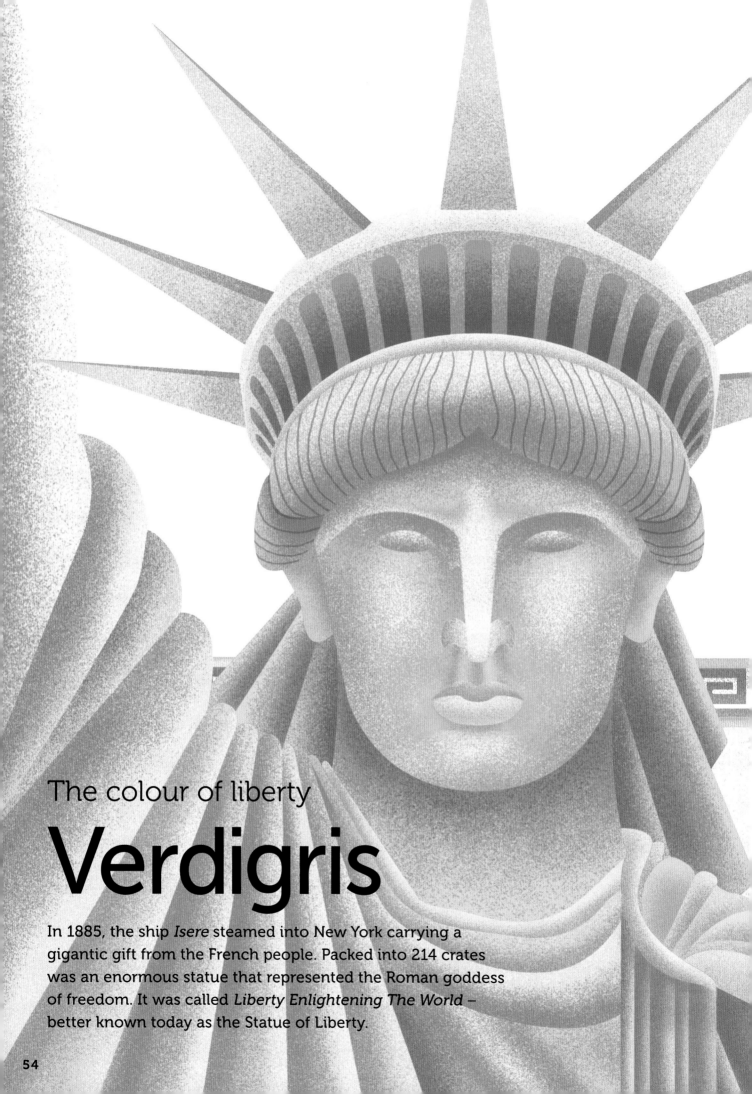

The colour of liberty

Verdigris

In 1885, the ship *Isere* steamed into New York carrying a
gigantic gift from the French people. Packed into 214 crates
was an enormous statue that represented the Roman goddess
of freedom. It was called *Liberty Enlightening The World* –
better known today as the Statue of Liberty.

Going green

The statue was assembled the following year on Bedloe's Island. Its 350 hand-beaten copper plates were fitted over the statue's iron frame and fastened in place. The statue started out a dull copper-brown colour, but within 20 years it had turned light green-blue. Reactions with the air and water had caused a thin layer, called a patina, to form on the surface of the copper. The material – and the colour – was called 'verdigris'.

Protective tarnish

Concerns about the statue's change of colour saw the US Congress raise US$62,000 to paint it in 1906, but the plans outraged many. Studies by US Army engineers concluded that the covering of verdigris actually helped protect the remaining copper underneath from further damage, so the statue was left alone. Copper-clad and domed buildings in many other cities have been left to tarnish in this way.

"Go down to Bedloe's Island and study the Statue of Liberty. You will find the most beautiful example of metal colouring in existence in the world today."

AMERICAN ARCHITECT STANFORD WHITE, 1906

Green from Greece

Verdigris occurs naturally due to weathering, but it was also made as a colouring. It gets its name from the French for 'green of Greece'. Ancient Greeks used to manufacture this pigment by placing thin slivers of copper in pots with sour wine or vinegar and leaving them to stand for weeks at a time. The patina that formed on the copper was scraped off and turned into a paint. It later proved popular with artists including Raphael, Titian and Jan Van Eyck.

The colour of rebellion
Irish and Kelly Green

Saint Patrick brought Christianity to Ireland in the 5th century and on his feast day, 17th March, celebrations abound in Ireland and elsewhere. People wear green clothing and symbols such as the shamrock clover leaf.

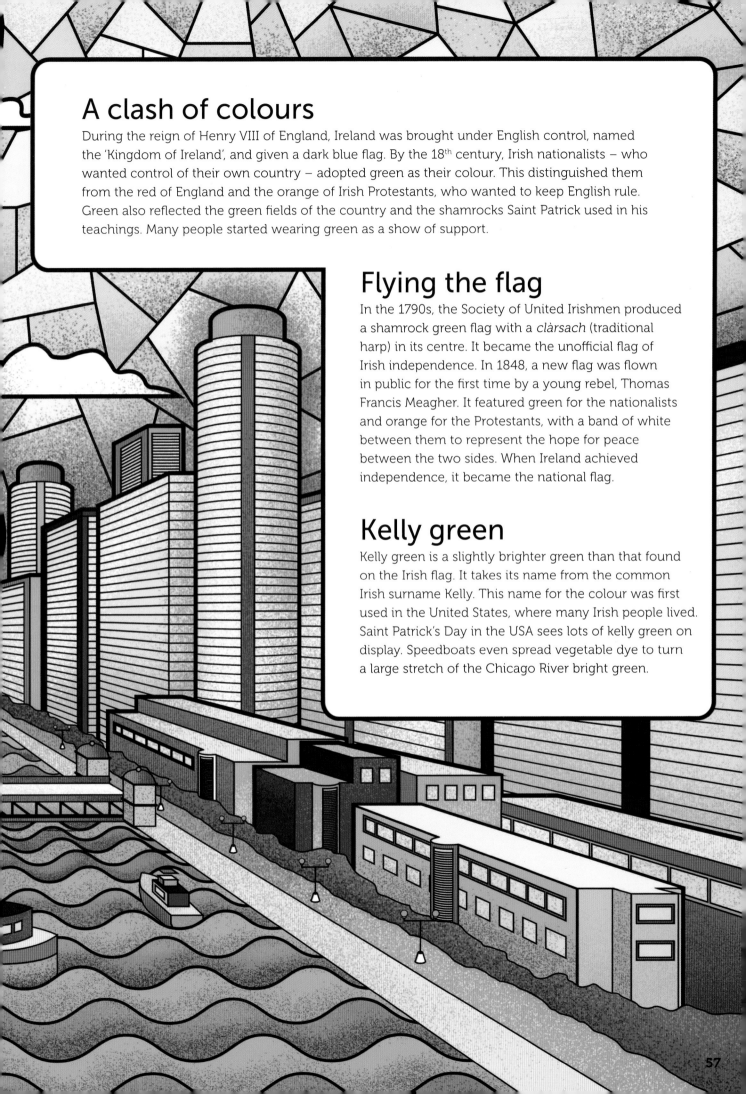

A clash of colours

During the reign of Henry VIII of England, Ireland was brought under English control, named the 'Kingdom of Ireland', and given a dark blue flag. By the 18th century, Irish nationalists – who wanted control of their own country – adopted green as their colour. This distinguished them from the red of England and the orange of Irish Protestants, who wanted to keep English rule. Green also reflected the green fields of the country and the shamrocks Saint Patrick used in his teachings. Many people started wearing green as a show of support.

Flying the flag

In the 1790s, the Society of United Irishmen produced a shamrock green flag with a *clàrsach* (traditional harp) in its centre. It became the unofficial flag of Irish independence. In 1848, a new flag was flown in public for the first time by a young rebel, Thomas Francis Meagher. It featured green for the nationalists and orange for the Protestants, with a band of white between them to represent the hope for peace between the two sides. When Ireland achieved independence, it became the national flag.

Kelly green

Kelly green is a slightly brighter green than that found on the Irish flag. It takes its name from the common Irish surname Kelly. This name for the colour was first used in the United States, where many Irish people lived. Saint Patrick's Day in the USA sees lots of kelly green on display. Speedboats even spread vegetable dye to turn a large stretch of the Chicago River bright green.

Dazzling but deadly

Scheele's Green

Carl Sheele made many scientific discoveries, but he was slow to publish his results. This meant that other chemists got the credit for many of Scheele's discoveries. Today, he is mostly remembered for inventing a bright but lethal colour.

Fatal fashion

These greens were soon found in thousands of homes, especially in Britain. Curtains, wallpaper and coloured paper dyed with emerald and Scheele's green were hugely popular. The dyes were also used in clothing, from high-fashion headdresses to humble socks. They were even used to colour sweets and other foods. But these colours came at a cost. The poisonous arsenic they contained was often absorbed by the body, causing headaches, sores and scabs – and even death. Gradually, the use of these greens diminished, although Scheele's green was used as an insecticide by US farmers in the 1930s.

Colour chemist

Scheele was a German pharmacist working in Sweden who loved nothing more than to conduct chemistry experiments late into the night. In the 1770s he discovered manganese, barium and oxygen, which he called 'fire air'. In 1775, Scheele invented a new green colour that contained copper and arsenic. Scheele's green was cheap to make, so it became popular. This led to the development of rival green pigments made in similar ways, including emerald green.

Death of an emperor?

After his defeat, French emperor Napoleon Bonaparte was sent into exile on a tiny island called Saint Helena. There, he lived in rooms decorated with paint and wallpaper in his favourite colour – green. Napoleon died in 1821, probably of stomach cancer, but the high levels of arsenic found in his body may have speeded up his decline.

"She actually carries in her skirts poison enough to slay the whole of the admirers she may meet with in half a dozen ball-rooms."

THE BRITISH MEDICAL JOURNAL IN 1862, WRITING ABOUT WEARERS OF ARSENIC GREEN DRESSES

Kohl Black and Graphite

Black was part of prehistoric people's palettes, as they used charcoal to write and draw with. Many blacks, such as kohl and graphite, come from rocky minerals which are either used in their solid form or ground down into powder and mixed with other substances.

Kohl black

Kohl was first used more than 5,000 years ago in ancient Egypt, where men and women drew thick lines of kohl around their eyes. It stopped their eyes being dazzled by the sun, but they also believed it had magical protective powers. Poorer people made kohl from soot mixed with animal fat. The wealthy made a better version from crushed galena or other minerals mixed with oils and precious metals – and sometimes scented with frankincense.

Graphite

Graphite is a grey-black form of carbon that can be easily drawn with and rubbed out using an eraser. In the past, graphite was so valuable that mines were guarded and miners flogged with whips if they were caught stealing any of the precious substance. Some graphite was sawn off into square sticks, wrapped in string or sheepskin and used as an easy writing and drawing tool. People thought it was a type of lead and called it 'plumbago' or 'black lead'. Graphite pencils are still known as 'lead pencils' today.

Pencil power

When a war meant that the French could no longer import solid graphite from England, Nicolas-Jacques Conté came up with an alternative. He mixed graphite powder with clay to form narrow rods, which he baked in an oven. He then placed each rod in two halves of a cylinder made of wood. The modern pencil was born! By varying the amount of clay and graphite, Conté made pencils of different blackness and hardness. His grading system from 9B (the softest and blackest) to 9H (the hardest) is still used in Europe today.

A colour to die for
Lime and Lead White

The colour of snow, milk, innocence and purity, whites made using metals or powdered rock have been used for thousands of years.

Lime white

Early people used chalk, a naturally-occurring form of limestone, to add highlights or white backgrounds to their cave paintings. Lime white was made from grinding chalk into a fine powder. Mixing it with salt and water made a thin paint called 'whitewash'. Whitewash was used to spruce up buildings and to seal the stones of the new home of the US President in 1798. This gave the building its name: the White House. The paint is still applied to the trunks of some fruit trees to stop the tree bark being damaged by large changes of temperature in winter.

Lead white

The White House was re-whitewashed several times until 1818, when the building was painted using a different material. Lead white was not new; it had been made for over 3,000 years in roughly the same way. Lead was allowed to react with vinegar in clay pots that were sealed and insulated with animal dung. After days or weeks, flakes of white formed on the vinegar's surface. It was scraped off and turned into a thick paint.

White wood, white faces

Artists liked lead white because it stuck to canvases and wood, and mixed easily with oil paints. Some shipbuilders used it to waterproof the timbers of wooden vessels. In the 17th century, lead white was used as make-up to give women pale white faces. But lead white is poisonous. Warnings about its dangers were first made in ancient times, but people still used the dangerous pigment. Some women lost their hair and teeth and suffered breathing problems. Artists such as Michelangelo, Goya and Caravaggio may have been made ill by the lead white they used in their paintings.

Index